The Art of Agreement

School of the Spirit Series

By
Grant Gomez

Unless otherwise indicated, all Scripture quotations are taken from the *KING JAMES VERSION* of the Bible.

Scripture quotations marked (AMP) are taken from the *Amplified® Bible*, Copyright © 1954, 1958, 1962, 1964, 1965, 1987 by The Lockman Foundation. Used by permission. (www.Lockman.org)

Scripture quotations marked (MSG Bible) are taken from *The Message*. Copyright © 1993, 1994, 1995, 1996, 2000, 2001, 2002. Used by permission of NavPress Publishing Group.

Definitions taken from *Strong's Exhaustive Concordance* unless otherwise indicated.

River of Life Revival Ministries
P.O. Box 510416
Punta Gorda, FL 33951
www.river4u.org
www.facebook.com/GrantGomezRevival
www.youtube.com/user/runswiththewind58
www.soundcloud.com/grantgomez

Contents

Chapter 1
Agreement - The Foundation

Verily I say unto you, Whatsoever ye shall bind on earth shall be bound in heaven; and whatsoever ye shall loose on earth shall be loosed in heaven. Again I say unto you, That if two of you shall agree on earth as touching any thing that they shall ask, it shall be done for them of my Father which is in heaven. For where two or three are gathered together in my name, there am I in the midst of them.
(Matthew 18:18-20)

The definition of agreement, based upon **Matthew 18:18-20**, comes from the Greek word *sumphoneo* which means to be in harmony; to accord; make a compact or stipulate. It's from a root word that means **harmonious or sounding together**. Practically applying, it means a consent or contract. Jesus actually taught us that **giving voice** to the Word of God **in unison** brings forth the manifestation.

Can two walk together, except they be agreed?
(Amos 3:3)

In this scripture, the Hebrew word for *agreed* means to fix upon; as a vision and to make contract in an assembly or gathering. This passage is talking about not just being together in existence but **being as one in vision and purpose**. You can't accomplish anything without being in agreement. God the Father, God the Son, and God the Holy Spirit had to walk together in agreement in order to bring about creation. God began creation with an agreement and created man by the

1

agreement of the Trinity to *Let Us make man in our image...* (**Genesis 1:26**). Notice the word ***our***.

Called to Agreement

God don't force us to agree. **He calls us to agree.** Obeying God is vital to our lives and is essential in marriage. Remember what God joins, he does not destroy. As the Word says in **Matthew 19:6**, *...What therefore God has joined together, let not man put asunder (separate)* (**Matthew 19:4-6,** AMP).

We learn that the Lord **empowers** us in agreement to do all He calls us to do. What is established in the spirit will manifest in the natural including a successful marriage. Being out of agreement with God affects **EVERY** area of our life.

The First Attack

The **first attack** the enemy brought **was upon agreement**. Satan understood the incredible power of agreement.

> *Now the serpent was more subtle than any beast of the field which the Lord God had made. And he said unto the woman, Yea, hath God said, Ye shall not eat of every tree of the garden?...*
> (**Genesis 3:1-6**)

Satan used deception to force a division between Adam and Eve. Adam chose to disagree with God by agreeing with the lie Eve had believed. The outcome of this disagreement set in motion the eventual destruction of the Garden of Eden, the breaking apart of the first family, and most importantly, the death of all mankind. Outsiders, Satan in this case, can detect a weakness within an Agreement. Just as in the Garden of Eden, the enemy comes to bring division and confusion in the marriage.

Agreement - The Marriage Covenant

†Point of Wisdom: Marriage is a life of giving not getting. It is not 50/50. It is designed to be 100% for both. The nature of giving guards agreement.

Our spouse is not a possession but a part of our being. It is impossible to have a "single person anointing" when married. **The greatest Power of God manifests as we begin to prefer one another**. Insisting on your way is not agreement. When you decide to agree you place things within Gods hands and it gets done. You sow the seed of agreement and the Lord will multiply the seed sown.

Agreement in Family

The 60's were the decade of division, liberal doctrine, and assault on family. We were told the lie of the "Generation Gap" where adults are unable to communicate with the younger generation. This was an attack on family and all authority thus hindering the destiny of future generations.

> In the same way you married men should live considerately with [your wives], with an intelligent recognition [of the marriage relation], honoring the woman as [physically] the weaker, but [realizing that you] are joint heirs of the grace (God's unmerited favor) of life, in order that your prayers may not be hindered and cut off. [Otherwise you cannot pray effectively.]
> (**1 Peter 3:7**, AMP)

Decisions that husbands and wives cannot agree upon should be set aside until the Lord brings an agreement between them. In **1 Peter 3:7**, the Word tells the husband to honor his wife. The word *honor* in the Greek is the word *timē* which means value, esteem

3

of the highest degree, give great dignity to. You can say that to honor something is to view it as costly, precious, most dear, valuable, and beloved. When that's in place, then agreement is easy. In fact, **honor is a form of agreement**.

> *Train up a child in the way he should go: and when he is old, he will not depart from it.*
> (**Proverbs 22:6**)

We raise, train, and provide for our children. Agreement is order - children are not teenagers and teenagers are not adults. Maturity is developed in an environment of agreement and consistency. **KIDS DON'T RAISE PARENTS.** If children can cause parents to disagree on an issue, then authority is broken down and rebellion can operate.

> *Except the Lord build the house, they labour in vain that build it....* (**Psalm 127:1**)

> *Thy wife shall be as a fruitful vine by the sides of thine house: thy children like olive plants round about thy table.* (**Psalm 128:3**)

†**Point of Wisdom:** God builds our homes, families, and futures as we are in agreement with Him. Peace reigns throughout our generations for years and we leave a legacy in the earth.

Chapter 2
Agreement - The Structure

Problems in the modern church started in the home. When there is a **breakdown in agreement**, there is a **ripple effect**. God is in the business of repairing foundations in order to heal the breech in the structure of society. Stop what affects the peace at home and you will stop what affects the peace in the church. When the church moves and operates in agreement, the Kingdom of God can be established.

> *Wives, submit yourselves unto your own husbands, as unto the Lord. For the husband is the head of the wife, even as Christ is the head of the church: and he is the saviour of the body.*
> **(Ephesians 5:22-23)**

Church is family and community. Paul teaches of the significance of **agreement by submission**. Submission does not mean slavery or sub-servitude, but means laying down one's agendas in agreement to fulfill a God-given purpose. This brings blessing and increase to us and honor and glory to God. A strong church body can withstand the attacks and assaults that come from the enemy. If a chain has a weak link, the chain is useless no matter how strong the other links are. **Agreement makes the church a strong CHAIN that can't be broken**.

Agreement in Destiny

And he gave some, apostles; and some, prophets; and some, evangelists; and some, pastors and teachers; For the perfecting of the saints, for the work of the ministry, for the edifying of the body of Christ: Till we all come in the unity of the faith... (**Ephesians 4:11-13**)

†Point of Wisdom: God releases destiny through Leadership. God places overseers, mentors, and parents in our life to speak, guide, and lead. It behooves us to glean from their wisdom and experience.

Parents are the prophetic voice of destiny to children just as the Five-Fold/Ascension Gift Ministries are the prophetic voice of destiny within the church. When we cannot agree with authority and wisdom, we lose focus and power. Accountability is another aspect of agreement. Along with this, we can Honor our leadership by Agreement. As we give honor, we are honored by God.

The definition of Spiritual Authority is something that has been delegated from a superior. Breakdown in this comes when we have the mindset of no superior. **Agreement with leadership is essential to defeating the works of the devil**.

Protecting Agreement

Keep thy heart with all diligence; for out of it are the issues of life (**Proverbs 4:23**)

A **guarded heart is not a closed heart**, instead it is an open and trusting heart. Allowing trust is a process that will take years of maturing. Our **trust** in God is **essential to Agreement**. Many times, past betrayals and hurts cause us to close our hearts to others and to God; therefore, the process of healing must take place before we are able to trust.

But I tell you, on the day of judgment men will have to give account for every idle (inoperative, non-working) word they speak. For by your words you will be justified and acquitted, and by your words you will be condemned and sentenced. (**Matthew 12:36-37**, AMP)

Our speech and confession will reinforce our agreement. Many people renew their marriage vows to each other before witnesses. We use the same principle by **SAYING** our **Agreement** and giving life to our faith.

So faith comes by hearing [what is told], and what is heard comes by the preaching [of the message that came from the lips] of Christ, (the Messiah Himself). (**Romans 10:17**, AMP)

This scripture declares that faith comes as we hear the Word of God. We apply the Agreement of Truth by our speech. This also reminds us of our Agreement and helps to hold us in accountability to it.

Persistence and commitment are the fruit of Agreement. We set example and lifestyle patterns as we continue in agreement. "Church hopping" in Christianity today is as common as divorce because of the lack of understanding of **Covenant**. Statistics in America report the average Christian lasts 7 years in attending a church before quitting. Many have lost their vision and destiny.

7

We are to be **assignment oriented** rather than need oriented. During the honeymoon period, there is Bliss. Many will say, "I need a church to meet my needs" because they are focused on themselves rather than on God. Remember, the Lord will lead us to the right church and place us there, if we follow His Voice. When relationships are based upon trust, giving, agreement, and covenant, they are strong against the attacks of this world.

> †**Point of Wisdom:** Remember, the enemy checks our persistence. He is very persistent himself. He never quits. He operates in agreement with Steal, Kill, and Destroy, and has been effective for thousands of years because of the **Power of Agreement.** According to Jesus, ... *Every kingdom divided against itself is brought to desolation; and every city or house divided against itself shall not stand: And if Satan cast out Satan, he is divided against himself; how shall then his kingdom stand?* (**Matthew 12:25-26**). Satan recognizes the power of agreement. So, if he operates and is successful in agreement, how much more should we?

Chapter 3
Agreement and the Anointing

Agreement is a bridge builder or connection to the anointing. The anointing carries everything we need to have a victorious life. It is the **channel of Blessing and Covenant**. Agreement causes us to be partakers of Blessing.

The **Sovereign Promises** of God are in effect regardless of whether we agree with them or not. These are the benefits of creation such as the earth and all that is within it; our seasons, cycles, and all that supports life. There is no need of Agreement in order to partake in what is provided by creation. God gives and we live. He is Creator without our approval or agreement.

The **Covenant Promises** of God are that which have been established through a mutual agreement. For example, the Lord gave us opportunity to benefit from what He instituted at Calvary. It is not automatic. The work of Calvary must be agreed with in order for the benefits of it to take place.

> *According as his divine power hath given unto us all things that pertain unto life and godliness, through the knowledge of him that hath called us to glory and virtue: Whereby are given unto us exceeding great and precious promises: that by these ye might be partakers of the divine nature, having escaped the corruption that is in the world through lust.* (**2 Peter 1:3-4**)

†Point of Wisdom: We see the Lord is willing but will not force this Covenant upon us. Agreement is God's gift to us which enables us to tap into the Anointing. Remember, Faith and Agreement work closely as we receive from God.

Agreement with the Presence of God

As we enjoy the Presence of God, we are changed. We receive from Him and we become partakers of the Divine Nature. If we are uncomfortable in the anointing and church, then we are out of agreement with God. The Lord **gives us His anointing** but we have to **yield to it**.

You will show me the path of life; in Your presence is fullness of joy, at Your right hand there are pleasures forevermore.
(**Psalm 16:11**, AMP)

Worship is a catalyst for Agreement. It brings our spirit, soul, and body to a place of surrender. It is voluntary, not forced. Intimacy is developed and we are developed to trust. God inhabits praise, adoration, and worship. The fellowship and communion of the Holy Ghost strengthens us to fulfill our Purpose and Destiny.

†Point of Wisdom: Always reverence the Presence of God and you will maintain and increase the Anointing upon your life. Never take for granted the Manifest Presence of God.

Agreement and the Open Heaven

*Behold, How good and how pleasant it is for brethren to **dwell together in unity**! It is like the precious ointment upon the head, that ran down upon the beard, even Aaron's beard: that went down to the skirts of his garments; As the dew of Hermon, and as the dew that descended upon the mountains of Zion: for there the Lord **commanded the blessing**, even life for evermore.* (**Psalm 133**)

Unity causes the anointing to flow and division to go! God pours out His Anointing upon the unity of brethren. What God ordains, He will bless. Division steals power from our churches. We can expect God to be God in His fullness as we become in one accord as on the Day of Pentecost (**Acts 2:1-3**). In the same way today, the **knitting of hearts together** to Believe for the Promise of God causes an **outpouring of His Presence**.

According to the scripture in **Acts 4:29-31**, when the believers were assembled together and prayed, the place was shaken by the Power of God. They had one heart and one mind. Corporate prayer is an opportunity for Agreement. As we come together to pray, it is more than mental or philosophical discussions. We have many opinions, but to come into agreement in prayer means to set aside human thinking and search the Mind and Heart of God on any situation. **Opinions cost nothing, but Agreement is work**.

Be of the same mind one toward another. Mind not high things, but condescend to men of low estate. Be not wise in your own conceits. (**Romans 12:16**)

Agreement within the Godhead is our example of perfect unity. The Father, Son, and Holy Ghost function in different realms but accomplish one purpose. The Anointing of the Holy Ghost always agrees with the Word of God (not with the interpretation, tradition, theology, religion, or opinion of men).

> *For as the body is one, and hath many members, and all the members of that one body, being many, are one body: so also is Christ. For by one Spirit are we all baptized into one body, whether we be Jews or Gentiles, whether we be bond or free; and have been all made to drink into one Spirit.* (**1 Corinthians 12:12-13**)

This passage reveals to us unity and diversity are knit together through the presence of the Holy Spirit within the Body of Christ. **NO SPIRIT = NO UNITY**. Also in **John 17:20-23**, Jesus made no personal demands. He was on a mission. He recognized His purpose was to fulfill the Father's will and He never strayed from that mission. Jesus **protected** His agreement by only **focusing** on the **Father's Mission**. Vision is a key to remaining in Agreement. Without a vision, people perish and cast off restraint.

> *Where there is no vision [no redemptive revelation of God], the people perish...* (**Proverbs 29:18**, AMP)

Agreement and Healing - Danielle's Testimony

In the spring of 2005, I met Danielle during an outreach we were conducting in Sarasota, Florida. Her family began to attend our Revival Center in Fort Myers which was about 1½ hours south of their home. Danielle was 13 years old at the time and had severe Crohn's Disease which is incurable. Her weight and appearance was that of a 9 year old. Her father would sometimes have to carry her into a meeting to receive prayer as she was too sick to walk.

I began to lay hands on her to release the Anointing and pray for a miracle in every service. There were many times in which she laid on the floor of our facility with a pillow and blanket during the services in the Atmosphere of Worship. They would never miss a meeting unless Danielle was in the hospital. Many times Freda (my wife) and I would go to pray in their home as well as the times she was in the hospital. **We came into AGREEMENT with Danielle and her family for the Promise of Healing according to the Word of God.**

In 2006, Danielle began to show signs of improvement but still had setbacks. God had brought her to us and it was a privilege, honor, and responsibility to minister to her. It was not easy, convenient, or instantaneous... but, it was NOT IMPOSSIBLE! **Freda and I were in AGREEMENT, all of our Leadership at River of Life Revival Center was in Agreement, all our congregation was in AGREEMENT, and God was in AGREEMENT for Danielle to be healed.**

Week after week I would preach and teach the vision of TOTAL HEALING and then pray again. Every time we had a visiting minister or a Revival meeting, we made a point of having Danielle up front in the prayer line for a Touch from God. Although flare-ups and treatments were less and less, she had a setback in 2007 and her doctors suggested a surgery of removing a portion of her colon leaving her with a colostomy bag. **Danielle adamantly refused and stated "GOD PROMISED TO HEAL ME and our church is in Agreement for that**

to happen." She did get better and was released from the hospital after several treatments.

At one point during the many times of prayer at our church, someone approached me to say I should let it go and move on because visitors and new families feel uncomfortable by us focusing so much on Danielle being healed. My response was "What if she was your daughter? She needs our help and God had brought her here to be healed. We are in the healing ministry here not an entertainment center." I then suggested if this person could not agree then LEAVE... He and his family left.

Finally... in 2008 during a Sunday morning meeting, we were about to pray for Danielle as she had a rough few days. One of our team Evangelists, Melissa, had a Word from the Lord that THE YOKE IS DESTROYED TODAY!!! She then began to pray for Danielle and the Power of God was all over her and she fell to the floor crying and shaking which had happened many times but this was much more INTENSE. From that point on, Danielle came out of this disease and was totally healed. She began to gain weight with no more symptoms.

This healing took **3 years to happen**. Now, she is healthy, beautiful, and happy... Now, she prays for people and they are healed. She recently visited our home and she talked about the POWER OF AGREEMENT and how God healed her even when it looked like it was never gonna happen. **God does His part, but we must CONTINUE in AGREEMENT until it happens**. She is one of many who have seen the Art of Agreement in operation for Healing.

Agreement is not Automatic

...Write the vision, and make it plain upon tables, that he may run that readeth it. For the vision is yet for an appointed time, but at the end it shall speak, and not lie: though it tarry, wait for it; because it will surely come, it will not tarry. Behold, his soul which is lifted up is not upright in him: but the just shall live by his faith.
(Habakkuk 2:2-4)

Vision must be preached. As we **give voice to vision** in our family, church, ministries, and career, we can **remain on track**. Focus can only come when there is something to see. We see in **Colossians 3:1-2** that we are to set our minds and affections on the things of God. Vision must be pursued in order to manifest agreement.

> **†Point of Wisdom:** Tunnel Vision can't see the Big Picture. God can't funnel the Big Picture through Tunnel Vision - Let God give you His Vision in order to see the Big Picture.

This brings us to an important principle called **PURPOSE**. The Lord wants us to do things on PURPOSE - Not accidental. The work of Calvary had a purpose. As we see our destiny before us, we have revelation of the Eternal Purpose of our personal life. **Ephesians 2** declares us to be God's workmanship, His building, temple, and dwelling place. We were ordained to build and be built. We are to reveal the Mystery of God to the world.

Also to enlighten all men and make plain to them what is the plan [regarding the Gentiles and providing for the salvation of all men] of the mystery kept hidden through the ages and concealed until now in [the mind of] God Who created all things by Christ Jesus. [The purpose is] that through the church the complicated, many-sided wisdom of God in all its infinite variety and innumerable aspects might now be made known to the angelic rulers and authorities (principalities and powers) in the heavenly sphere. This is in accordance with the terms of the eternal and timeless purpose which He has realized and carried into effect in [the person of] Christ Jesus our Lord...

(**Ephesians 3:9-11**, AMP)

God wants to shine through us and Agreement makes that happen!

The Oneness Jesus prayed for is the Active Kingdom of God on Earth. Oneness manifested is agreement. Our anointing is at its peak of power when agreement is in place. The work of God in the earth shall **RISE** upon His people as the manifestation of **GLORY** in these last days.

Arise, Shine; for thy light is come, and the glory of the Lord is risen upon thee... (**Isaiah 60:1-3**)

Because of this glory, the world will be drawn to Jesus. God wants the knowledge of His glory in all the earth, and to cover all the earth as it was said by the prophet Habakkuk (**Habakkuk 2:14**). This will be done through his people.

Satanic attack is upon the building of the Kingdom and its Workers. The enemy will attack our fruit production. The **lack of fruit** is always a **hindrance to Agreement**. As demonic assault comes on the Workers of God, there is division, lost focus, confusion, and discouragement. So many times we are led astray by offense. Here we are vulnerable and weak because of isolation. One battle tactic the devil will use is **DIVIDE and CONQUER**. In this the enemy does not have to get us into the bondage of sin, just stop us from the Kingdom work and delay our destiny unto Victory.

†Point of Wisdom: When problems arise, RUN TO GOD - RUN TO CHURCH - RUN TO PRAYER - RUN TO THE WORD - RUN TO YOUR PASTOR, but do not RUN AWAY!!! Give up the Low Life in exchange for the High Life. Become a Kingdom Seeker.

Allow the Lord to show you points of agreement where you can line up with His will and begin to operate under the Open Heaven and Power of His Anointing. Ask God to give you a fresh vision for your life. Ask him for a fresh touch and renewal. Take time to SOAK in His Presence and listen. Let Him heal old hurts and betrayals that have poisoned your heart from Unity and Agreement. I pray the Lord release His Anointing upon your life right now that you be drawn to Him. I **AGREE** with you for victory in Jesus name.

Chapter 4
Keeping Agreement in Place

You will guard him and keep him in perfect and constant peace whose mind [both its inclination and its character] is stayed on You, because he commits himself to You, leans on You and hopes confidently in You.   (**Isaiah 26:3**, AMP)

Peace keeps Agreement in Place. Peace inward will cause peace outward. The fruit of peace is grown as we face adversity. The peace of God enables us to hold on to a promise. We trust God and so we can rest in the place of Agreement. When we are at peace with God, we are at peace with others.

†**Point of Wisdom:** You don't overcome thoughts with thoughts; You overcome thoughts with **words**. Faith comes by hearing the Word of God. That means even repeating it to yourself over and over until your mind is renewed.

Jesus said unto him, Thou shalt love the Lord thy God with all thy heart, and with all thy soul, and with all thy mind. This is the first and great commandment. And the second is like unto it, Thou shalt love thy neighbour as thyself. On these two commandments hang all the law and the prophets.   (**Matthew 22:37-40**)

Love will cause Agreement to be reinforced over and over. Because we love God, we will stay in Agreement with Him. When we stay in Agreement with Him, it is easy to stay in Agreement with His people. The Lord wants us to have an understanding of Unity with Him. He wants us to have an understanding of Unity with each other. To have one purpose we must have one mind. **1 Corinthians 1:9-10** declares to us that to be perfectly joined we must have one mind. To have the same mind there must be a standard. The Word of God is the Mind and Heart of God. **Agreement** and **Unity** will be in place as we **submit to the Word**.

> *For the love of Christ constraineth us...*
> (**2 Corinthians 5:14**)

The Greek word for *constraineth* is *sunecho* which means to hold together, i.e. to compress. In other words, the love of God will hold us in a place of Agreement.

Agreement and Discipleship

We are disciples of Christ. We were chosen by God and designed by Him to submit to His training and care. A disciple is more than a pupil. He is a part of his master. There has to be a yielded and teachable spirit in the true disciple.

> *Go then and* ***make*** *disciples of all the nations, baptizing them into the name of the Father and of the Son and of the Holy Spirit, Teaching them to observe everything that I have commanded you...* (**Matthew 28:19-20**, AMP)

The Great Commission is not the Great Suggestion. The Lord commands us to **MAKE** disciples. Discipleship means to be under discipline and mentorship. A **disciple** has to **agree** with the **teacher**. You cannot make a disciple unless they are committed to the process of growth.

Herein is my Father glorified, that ye bear much fruit; so shall ye be my disciples. (**John 15:8**)

Jesus in **John 15:1-8** tells us that remaining attached (in Agreement) with Him will cause us to grow and bear fruit. He also declares the Father is glorified in that we bear the true marks of a disciple.

Training and Equipping is something mutual for the sake of something eternal. A disciple is trained to be all and more than the teacher. God never releases more to us than our level of commitment to Agreement with Him. **As we are faithful to the little matters, God gives us greater responsibility**.

> **†Point of Wisdom:** I have learned over many years the faithfulness of God to promote those who are faithful in another man's ministry. God desires us to learn through submission in order to carry great responsibility.

He that is faithful in that which is least is faithful also in much: and he that is unjust in the least is unjust also in much. If therefore ye have not been faithful in the unrighteous mammon, who will commit to your trust the true riches? And if ye have not been faithful in that which is another man's, who shall give you that which is your own? No servant can serve two masters: for either he will hate the one, and love the other; or else he will hold to the one, and despise the other. Ye cannot serve God and mammon.
(**Luke 16:10-13**)

Although this is used as a teaching on money, the principle is faithfulness, honor, and agreement. We see that we cannot serve two masters. The Lord asks for Agreement in order to help us personally. Jesus speaks of "True Riches." This speaks of a price that has to be paid in order to possess the Kingdom.

Agreement and the Law of Impartation

For I am yearning to see you, that I may impart and share with you some spiritual gift to strengthen and establish you...
                              (**Romans 1:11,** AMP)

Here Paul speaks of the ministry of impartation being important. Impartation is a key to maturing spiritually. There has to be **agreement for impartation to be effective** in the life of a Christian. We recognize that Jesus released spiritual things to his disciples as they were continually in association with Him. The Laying on of Hands is one way of giving, but the person receiving has to enter into agreement with the one ministering.

...Believe in the Lord your God, so shall ye be established; believe his prophets, so shall ye prosper.   (**2 Chronicles 20:20**)

We should believe the one whom God sends to our life to minister to us. It is not "man worship" to come into agreement with Leadership. Always follow Faith, Fruit, and Anointing when submitting and yielding to Leaders. It is essential for us to have healthy relationships within the church. I always say, "**If you can't agree - get out of the way.**" We could hinder the growth or victory of others by our lack of agreement. There is more power to have 3 people in agreement than 300 undecided and divided.

I BESEECH you therefore, brethren, by the mercies of God, that ye present your bodies a living sacrifice, holy, acceptable unto God, which is your reasonable service. And be not conformed to this world: but be ye transformed by the renewing of your mind, that ye may prove what is that good, and acceptable, and perfect, will of God.   (**Romans 12:1-2**)

This passage of scriptures admonishes us to continually present ourselves to the Lord as a living sacrifice. This will help us to receive all He has for us. God's will is to conform us into His image. **Agreement makes us a reflection of what we agree with**. Jesus was the express image of the Father because he was in perfect agreement with Him.

Receiving Instructions

These are some practical keys to help us in receiving impartation from the Lord.

- **1 Corinthians 12:1-13** - Drinking as a partaker joined with Christ
- **Romans 8:1-17** - Yielding through adoption
- **Ephesians 5:15-21** - Drinking to overflow
- **Mark 6:53-56** - The power of hunger and touch
- **Galatians 3:1-9** - Receiving corporately (by faith)
- **Matthew 5:1-10** - The BE attitudes of a blessing
- **John 7:37** - Coming to Jesus
- **Psalm 64:1-7** - Longing, praising, soaking, and meditating
- **Isaiah 40:28-31** - Waiting on the Lord
- **Hebrews 4:9-10** - Entering into the REST
- **Psalm 16:11** - The Presence of God - the Glory of God
- **Psalm 92:10-15** - The Fresh Oil from Heaven given

Agreement and Partnership

I have planted, Apollos watered; but God gave the increase. So then neither is he that planteth any thing, neither he that watereth; but God that giveth the increase. Now he that planteth and he that watereth are one: and every man shall receive his own reward according to his own labour. For we are labourers together with God: ye are God's husbandry, ye are God's building.
(**1 Corinthians 3:6-9**)

We see we are **God's fellow workers** and we **enter into an agreement with Him to do a work** in the earth. We are building His Kingdom, but we are receiving the benefits of that Kingdom through that partnership. The Lord does not leave us alone in our assignment but aids us through the contract by sealing us with the Holy Ghost.

†Point of Wisdom: God is not looking for servants. He is looking for partnership. We are not His employees. We are His family, His children. We work with Him, not for Him.

We are stewards of the Mystery of God as it says in **1 Corinthians 4:1-2**. We reveal Jesus in the earth to all. It is important to be in agreement with the One we represent. God is not pleased by "False Advertising" and "Misrepresentation." The Lord wants us found faithful. This speaks of agreement and partnership. God never has a problem upholding His agreement with us.

Do not be unequally yoked up with unbelievers [do not make mismatched alliances with them, or come under a different yoke with them, inconsistent with your faith]...
(**2 Corinthians 6:14**, AMP)

This speaks of an "unequal yoke" that Christians can enter into. The word *yoke* is another term for

Partnership. We see the dangers of this illustration and understand there is also an **EQUAL YOKE** we enter into **with the Lord**. He will also come beside us in His things as our Helper.

> *Likewise the Spirit also **helpeth** our infirmities: for we know not what we should pray for as we ought: but the Spirit itself **maketh intercession** for us with groanings which cannot be uttered. And he that searcheth the hearts knoweth what is the mind of the Spirit, because he **maketh intercession** for the saints according to the will of God.* (**Romans 8:26-27**)

The word *helpeth* in this passage is the Greek word *sunantilambanomai* which means to take hold of opposite together, i.e. co-operate (assist:)-help. This is the promise of God taking hold of together with us in prayer and intercession. **Within partnership there is a connection in the Spirit with God and each other**. Many times we see those in Partnership "Praying in the Spirit" for one another as the Lord moves upon them to do so even though they may be miles apart.

> *For even in Thessalonica you sent [me contributions] for my needs, not only once but a second time. Not that I seek or am eager for [your] gift, but I do seek and am eager for the fruit which increases to your credit [the harvest of blessing that is accumulating to your account]. But I have [your full payment] and more; I have everything I need and am amply supplied, now that I have received from Epaphroditus the gifts you sent me. [They are the] fragrant odor of an offering and sacrifice which God welcomes and in which He delights. And my God will liberally supply (fill to the full) your every need according to His riches in glory in Christ Jesus.* (**Philippians 4:16-19**, AMP)

God makes connections and networks for Kingdom growth. We are faithful to support our storehouse with His tithe, but giving in prayer and partnership with ministries is a response to God moving in our heart and is covenant (Agreement) minded. **The Lord connects us by agreement and partnership to support the work of the Kingdom**. We see this in the context of (**Philippians 4:19**) that God supplies every need to those in partnership with Paul's mission work in Thessalonica. He also commends his ministry partner Epaphroditus by saying the offering was pleasing to the Lord.

My wife and I have personally experienced this truth in our lives as we have traveled into impoverished areas to minister. The financial support and prayer partnership enables us to fulfill the call of God to these precious people. As we have stayed in covenant with our partners, we have seen the promises of God fulfilled in their lives and calls as well. They go with us into the harvest field whether they are physically present with us or not. The fruit of our ministry is not just preaching the Gospel to the lost, but also seeing our partners prosper and increase. Although we are blessed by our partners, God has always been our source and always will be.

As we are **faithful in our partnerships, God supplies our needs**. Partnership is a bridge for the Anointing and Blessing of ministries to be operative in your life. You sow seed and God brings your Harvest. This is the ultimate Agreement.

26

Chapter 5
Agreement Produces
Spiritual Champions

The thief cometh not, but for to steal, and to kill, and to destroy: I am come that they might have life, and that they might have it more abundantly. (**John 10:10**)

In this passage of scripture, *Jesus* taught that the **thief comes to steal, kill, and destroy.** To steal means to take possession of something through unlawful means. An outlaw must be captured and brought to justice before his deeds can be punished. As long as he eludes arrest he can continue stealing as well as murdering and destroying property.

Would you sit back and let a thief plunder your home, abuse your family, steal your valuables, and vandalize your property? I am sure you would not.

Although this book is for men and women alike, I have a word for husbands, fathers, and all men who care for their families. If a thief was attacking your family, some of the Good Ole Boys would take the shotgun, rifle, and the four wheel drive and go after the bad man cause ... *a Country Boy Can Survive*.[1] Well, I am in agreement with that. But what about the **Spiritual Bad Man**? He is a greater threat than the criminal on the street. But he is allowed to break up many homes with no resistance from Good Ole Boys. This is so evident today when you see all the husbands and fathers letting the wives and mothers take the children to church or teaching them to pray and worship God. I have heard many men over the years say "my wife's got enough religion for both of us." That's a cop out. It's **time to man-up and take responsibility** as the spiritual heads and leaders in our homes.

> *...God is strong, and He wants you strong. So take everything the Master has set out for you, well-made weapons of the best materials. And put them to use so you will be able to stand up to everything the devil throws your way. This is no afternoon athletic contest that we'll walk away from and forget about in a couple of hours. This is for keeps, a life-or-death fight to the finish against the devil and his angels. Be prepared. You're up against far more than you can handle on your own. Take all the help you can get, every weapon God has issued, so that when it's all over but the shouting you'll still be on your feet...* (**Ephesians 6:10-13**, MSG Bible)

Before I was saved I was in a lot of fights, brawls, and life-threatening situations involving guns, knives, or any other equalizer that gave me the edge. Because I was small in stature, I knew I had to hit first and not let them get up. It is nothing to boast about, but it is what it is. I would not think twice about protecting my wife and kids or any other family member or friend from a threat. When I got saved, the hostility and violence in my life changed. I soon became aware of the enemy of my soul. I began to see that the devil was after my family. But I could not stop him with a shotgun. A baseball bat or machete has no effect. If I threatened him with a 45, he would just laugh at me and come on in. I needed an **equalizer that would stop the devil**. I realized I had to be FILLED with the Power of the Holy Ghost!! He is more than an EQUALIZER - He is a DOMINATOR against the devil. **I had to come into Agreement with the Word of God and the Spirit of God in order to protect my family**.

†Point of Wisdom: Let us take heed to the Word and be the Champions for our families. Get between our loved ones and the **Spiritual Bad Man.** Do what it takes to get him out, and keep him out. Then go help somebody else fight him and win. Stay full of the Holy Ghost and there will be no room for anything else. Surrender to the Lord your life and you will save someone else. Take responsibility for protecting, providing, and praying for your family. Pray and ask God to develop you as a man or woman of God. Agree with the Word and Yield to the Spirit! **Yes... GO TO CHURCH MEETINGS but be the CHURCH AT HOME.**

Remember, a Spiritual Champion is one who wins battles. **Apart from Agreement with God, you can never win a battle**. It is my prayer that you win. I **AGREE** with you and the Word of God to be the Conqueror and Champion He has called you to be.

Notes

1. Hank Williams, Jr., *The Pressure Is On*, (Nashville, TN: Elektra/Curb Records, 1981).

School of the Spirit Series

He Gave Gifts

The Art of Agreement

Rewards of Revival

Suggested Books

Ever Increasing Faith by Smith Wigglesworth

Insights to the Anointing by Chris Harvey

Integrity - The Missing Ingredient by Carol Fuss

The Normal Christian Life by Watchman Nee

So I'm Out of Debt - What's Next? by Carol Fuss

Why Tongues? by Kenneth E. Hagin

Prayer for Salvation

Heavenly Father, I come to you in the name of Jesus. In **Romans 10:9-10** your Word says, *That if thou shalt confess with thy mouth the Lord Jesus, and shalt believe in thine heart that God hath raised him from the dead, thou shalt be saved.* I believe that Jesus died for my sins and was raised from the dead. Jesus, I ask you to come into my life and be my Lord and Savior. Forgive me of all my sins. I repent now and I confess with my mouth that Jesus is Lord. Jesus, You are now Lord of my life. (Say to the devil: Take your hands off my life and my future. I belong to God!) Jesus, I am yours and you are mine. Thank you for saving me.

Amen.

Receive the Baptism in the Holy Spirit

If you are born again or just received salvation from praying the above prayer, you are qualified to receive the baptism in the Holy Spirit. One of the evidences of the Holy Spirit is speaking in tongues as the Spirit gives you utterance according to **Acts 2:4. Luke 11:13** reads, *If ye then, being evil, know how to give good gifts unto your children: How much more shall your heavenly Father give the Holy Spirit to them that ask him?* If you are ready to receive the baptism in the Holy Spirit, pray this prayer...

Heavenly Father, I ask you according to **Luke 11:13** to fill me with your Holy Spirit. I expect to worship You with other tongues as the Holy Spirit gives me utterance according to **Acts 2:4**. Holy Spirit, I welcome you. Come fill me now.

Now begin to worship Him just as the scripture in **John 7:38** (AMP) says... *He who believes in Me - who cleaves to and trusts in and relies on Me - as the Scripture has said, Out from his innermost being springs and rivers of living water shall flow (continuously).* So, whatever sounds, songs, or words come out, let them flow.

Our Ministry Mandate

The Nation is desperate for a true move of God. We need a shaking that revives the weary and brings life to the dead. We need a shift that transforms culture, resurrects a cry for holiness, and rekindles a passion for the lost. We need an Awakening. We believe that this Awakening is here and is happening now! We have been seeing a people dissatisfied with the usual church hype and religious fads. They want to do more than just get excited; they want to change the world, and reach the Nations. We are dedicated to equipping all generations and cultures, setting them on fire for Jesus. It is time to touch God through raw worship, deep seeking intimacy, and the pure uncompromised Message of the Full Gospel of Jesus Christ. We know that just one touch - one encounter with the Real God - will change people forever!

"THERE IS NO HIGH LIKE THE MOST HIGH®."

-Grant and Freda Gomez

Contact Grant Gomez for ministry at:
P.O. Box 510416
Punta Gorda, FL 33951
www.river4u.org